This journal belongs to...

_____

If found, please contact:

_____

_____

Copyright @ 2023 The Kaizen Company

ISBN 979-889298423-2
US $39.99
53999

9 798892 984232

STRIVE FOR PROGRESS

The Kaizen Journal

Kai - Change   Zen - Good

kai - zen

Japanese

(n.) The philosophy of constant improvement.
Every day is an opportunity to improve.

It's not about being invincible, it's about being
unstoppable

"Everyone wants to live on top of the mountain, but all the happiness and growth occurs while you're climbing it."

Andy Rooney

Welcome to the transformative journey meant to help you achieve your most audacious dreams. This journal is a powerful tool meticulously crafted to guide you in embracing your unique strengths, and eliminating your self-doubt. The power to create the life you desire lies within you, and this journal is here to support and inspire you every step of the way.

Open your heart and mind, and let the pages of this journal be a testament to your growth, resilience, and the extraordinary journey that lies ahead.

Four Reasons

You Should

Complete This

Journal

Boosts Confidence and Eliminates your Self-Doubt

Imagine if you had a stack of undeniable proof that you are who you say you are. This journal serves that purpose. Imagine if you completed this journal from front to back. You would have 19 weeks worth of evidence that you will accomplish anything you say you are going to. Outwork your self-doubt.

Tracks your Progress and Keeps you Motivated

Journaling serves as a powerful tool for tracking your progress by providing a documented record of your thoughts, emotions, and experiences over time. As you consistently write in your journal, you can look back and compare past entries to see how far you've come in terms of personal growth, goals achieved, and challenges overcome. By reviewing your journal entries, you gain valuable insights into areas where you may need to make adjustments to continue progressing

Builds Discipline

Today discipline is extremely scarce; however, this is great news for you. In a world where mediocrity is so prevalent, this leaves you with loads of opportunity. This journal will hold you accountable, thus helping you stay disciplined. If you finished 19 weeks of learning new skills, meditating, and exercising, you will have established indestructible discipline,

Constructed Solely for Personal Growth

This journal is so powerful because it is completely constructed with the purpose to lead you towards becoming a part of the top 1% of people. The three priorities that you are left to complete every day are activities that almost all of the most successful people credit their success to. Meditation helps you stay focused and acquire mental clarity. Exercise helps boost your physical and mental well being, as well as keep you in shape. An hour towards learning helps you stay creative and helps boost cognitive function by challenging your brain. Journaling helps you reflect on your day and declutter your mind, as well as helping you track your progress. Lastly, by listing what you're grateful for, you will live a much happier lifestyle.

Why Is There Three Wins To Complete Every Day?

Why should I Complete the 3 Wins?

This journal was built off of the philosophy that you just need to get one percent better every single day. No days should go to waste. If you have proof everyday that you did one thing that challenged you mentally, physically, and spiritually for the duration of this journal, you would have twenty weeks of consistent self-improvement under your belt.

The only difference between those who are great and those who are average is discipline. This journal will help ensure that you stay on track and help you prove to yourself that you are exactly who you say you are. After these 19 weeks you will be smarter, fitter, more grateful, and have a higher sense of mental clarity as well as have 19 weeks of proof that you leveled up every single day. If you take away anything from this journal, it should be that you should complete three wins everyday. Good luck on this journey and remember… you don't have to be invincible, you just have to be unstoppable.

"Meditation brings wisdom; lack of meditation leaves ignorance. Know well what leads you forward and what holds you back, and choose the path that leads to wisdom."

Buddha

Why should I get a Spiritual Win

The concept of a "spiritual win" may vary depending on individual beliefs and practices. It does not matter if you achieve this spiritual win through prayer, meditation, affirmations, scriptures and passages, or other practices, if you consistently achieve a spiritual win it will possess several benefits.

It will offer inner peace and clarity through the process of regularly connecting with one's spiritual self and provide a daily reset which can help reduce stress and anxiety. A spiritual win will also help you stay true to your path of leveling up by reaffirming your core moral and ethical values . Lastly the spiritual win can provide you with an outlet to practice gratitude by showing appreciation for life's blessings.

It's important to note that spirituality is a deeply personal and individual experience, and what constitutes a "spiritual win" can vary greatly from person to person. What's essential is finding practices and beliefs that resonate with you personally and contribute to your overall well-being and growth.

"Exercise is a vehicle of transformation, not only for your body but also for your mind and spirit."

Jillian Michaels

Why should I get a Physical Win?

Exercise is the key to building your foundation and is apparent when looking at all of the most high value people. You don't have to constantly put your body through hell every single day to reap the benefits, you just have to take some time to prioritize your health. It can be a light jog, some yoga, a game of pick up, or just walking your dog.

Exercise is essential for maintaining a healthy lifestyle as it improves cardiovascular health, strengthens muscles and bones, and enhances flexibility and balance. Regular physical activity also helps manage weight, reduce the risk of chronic diseases, and boost overall immune function. Additionally, exercise releases endorphins, promoting a positive mood and reducing stress, ultimately contributing to better mental well-being. Also it will ensure your quality of living, if you don't use your joints now, you definitely won't as you get older.

Lastly, it boosts your confidence and will build up your discipline. If you have the discipline to exercise every single day, there truly is nothing in this world you can't accomplish.

"Your growth is limited only by the extent of your willingness to expand your mind and embrace new possibilities."

John C. Maxwell

Why should I get a Mental Win?

Learning every day is vital because it fosters personal growth, expands knowledge and skills, and enables individuals to adapt to an ever-changing world. Continuous learning enhances critical thinking abilities, promotes creativity, and encourages curiosity, leading to a deeper understanding of oneself and the world. It empowers individuals to stay relevant, embrace new opportunities, and remain adaptable in both personal and professional realms.

How do you expect to think new thoughts if you think the way you've always thought. That's why you must make it a mission to set aside time everyday to challenge your mind by either reading, learning a new skill, or watching a video. There are no barriers to where you can draw inspiration from and there are a million different ways to learn.

The one thing separating you from the billions of others on this planet is your mind, no one thinks the way you think and that is a beautiful gift, don't waste it. You are truly unique and that is your super power, the world is constantly in need of innovation and you never know what you may be able to offer to this world.

Why should you Write your Long-Term Goals?

When it comes to setting goals, it becomes evident that no two people have the same aspirations and ambitions. Each person possesses a unique combination of experiences, values, passions, and dreams, leading to a personalized vision of what they want to achieve in life. Whether it's personal, professional, or spiritual growth, everyone's goals are shaped by their individual circumstances and desires.

This is why it is so important that you write your own individual aspirations inside this journal, some people just want to lose weight, while others may want to build up a social media following. Whatever it is, it is important that you keep that vision in the back of your head at all time and track your progress.

For instance if you are trying to become an influencer, make it a goal of yours every day to work towards that, and then track the amount of followers you have on your weekly updates. You will be shocked at how much progress you are making, thus keeping you motivated through out the journey. Imagine seeing how much progress you made towards your vision at the end of these 19 weeks. Good luck.

What are your longterm goals?

_____

_____

_____

_____

_____

Where are you at in those goals right now?

_____

_____

_____

_____

_____

_____ / _____ / _____

"It always seems impossible until it is done."
Nelson Mandela

Priorities:

Spiritual Win	Mental Win	Physical Win

Today's Checklist:

☐   ☐   ☐

☐   ☐   ☐

I am grateful for...

1. _____

2. _____

Daily Reflection

_____

_____

_____

_____

_____

_____

_____

_____ / _____ / _____

"You are never really playing an opponent. You are playing yourself, your own highest standards, and when you reach your limits, that is real joy."
Arthur Ashe

Priorities:

Spiritual Win	Mental Win	Physical Win

Today's Checklist:

☐   ☐   ☐

☐   ☐   ☐

I am grateful for...

1. _____
2. _____

Daily Reflection

_____
_____
_____
_____
_____
_____
_____

_____ / _____ / _____

Today's Affirmation:
I trust in the journey of life and have faith that everything happens for a
reason.

Priorities:

Spiritual Win	Mental Win	Physical Win

Today's Checklist:

☐   ☐   ☐

☐   ☐   ☐

I am grateful for...

1. _____

2. _____

Daily Reflection

_____

_____

_____

_____

_____

_____

_____

_____ / _____ / _____

"Success usually comes to those who are too busy to be looking for it."
Henry David Thoreau

Priorities:

Spiritual Win	Mental Win	Physical Win

Today's Checklist:

☐   ☐   ☐

☐   ☐   ☐

I am grateful for...

1. _____

2. _____

Daily Reflection

_____

_____

_____

_____

_____

_____

_____

_____ / _____ / _____

"Opportunities don't happen. You create them."
Chris Grosser

Priorities:

Spiritual Win	Mental Win	Physical Win

Today's Checklist:

☐ ☐ ☐

☐ ☐ ☐

I am grateful for...

1. _____

2. _____

Daily Reflection

_____
_____
_____
_____
_____
_____
_____

_____ / _____ / _____

"The road to success and the road to failure are almost exactly the same."
Colin R. Davis

Priorities:

Spiritual Win	Mental Win	Physical Win

Today's Checklist:

☐   ☐   ☐

☐   ☐   ☐

I am grateful for...

1. _____
2. _____

Daily Reflection

_____
_____
_____
_____
_____
_____
_____
_____

_____ / _____ / _____

"You gotta take a risk or you'll be doing the same shit forever."
Anonymous

Priorities:

Spiritual Win	Mental Win	Physical Win

Today's Checklist:

☐   ☐   ☐

☐   ☐   ☐

I am grateful for...

1. _____

2. _____

Daily Reflection

_____

_____

_____

_____

_____

_____

_____

Weekly Update

Goals for the Week:

☐ _____

☐ _____

☐ _____

What were your biggest accomplishments this week?

_____

_____

_____

_____

What areas could you have improved on this week?

_____

_____

_____

_____

_____ / _____ / _____

"A bend in the road is not the end of the road... unless
you fail to make the turn."
Helen Keller

Priorities:

Spiritual Win	Mental Win	Physical Win

Today's Checklist:

☐ ☐ ☐

☐ ☐ ☐

I am grateful for...

1. _____

2. _____

Daily Reflection

_____

_____

_____

_____

_____

_____

_____

_____ / _____ / _____

"A smooth sea never made a skilled sailor."
Franklin D. Roosevelt

Priorities:

Spiritual Win	Mental Win	Physical Win

Today's Checklist:

☐   ☐   ☐

☐   ☐   ☐

I am grateful for...

1. _____

2. _____

Daily Reflection

_____

_____

_____

_____

_____

_____

_____

_____/_____/_____

"You are the average of the five people you spend the most time with."
Jim Rohn

Priorities:

Spiritual Win	Mental Win	Physical Win

Today's Checklist:

☐   ☐   ☐

☐   ☐   ☐

I am grateful for...

1. _____
2. _____

Daily Reflection

_____

_____

_____

_____

_____

_____

_____

_____ / _____ / _____

"Perseverance is not a long race; it is many short races one after the other."
Walter Elliot

Priorities:

Spiritual Win	Mental Win	Physical Win

Today's Checklist:

☐ ☐ ☐

☐ ☐ ☐

I am grateful for...

1. _____

2. _____

Daily Reflection

_____
_____
_____
_____
_____
_____
_____
_____

_____ / _____ / _____

"Success is where preparation meets opportunity."
Zig Ziglar

Priorities:

Spiritual Win	Mental Win	Physical Win

Today's Checklist:

☐   ☐   ☐

☐   ☐   ☐

I am grateful for...

1. _____

2. _____

Daily Reflection

_____

_____

_____

_____

_____

_____

_____

_____

_____ / _____ / _____

"I hated every minute of training, but I said don't quit. Suffer now and live the rest of your life as a champion."
Muhammad Ali

Priorities:

Spiritual Win	Mental Win	Physical Win

Today's Checklist:

☐   ☐   ☐

☐   ☐   ☐

I am grateful for...

1. _____

2. _____

Daily Reflection

_____

_____

_____

_____

_____

_____

_____

_____ / _____ / _____

Today's Affirmation:
I am capable of achieving any goal I set my mind to.

Priorities:

Spiritual Win	Mental Win	Physical Win

Today's Checklist:

☐ ☐ ☐

☐ ☐ ☐

I am grateful for...

1. _____

2. _____

Daily Reflection

_____

_____

_____

_____

_____

_____

_____

_____

Weekly Update

Goals for the Week:

☐ _____

☐ _____

☐ _____

*What were your biggest
accomplishments this week?*

_____

_____

_____

_____

*What areas could you have
improved on this week?*

_____

_____

_____

_____

_____ / _____ / _____

Practice gratitude daily, for it is the key to
finding contentment and abundance.

Priorities:

Spiritual Win	Mental Win	Physical Win

Today's Checklist:

☐ ☐ ☐

☐ ☐ ☐

I am grateful for...

1. _____
2. _____

Daily Reflection

_____
_____
_____
_____
_____
_____
_____

_____ / _____ / _____

"Life begins at the end of your comfort zone."
Neale Donald Walsch

Priorities:

Spiritual Win	Mental Win	Physical Win

Today's Checklist:

☐   ☐   ☐

☐   ☐   ☐

I am grateful for...

1. _____

2. _____

Daily Reflection

_____

_____

_____

_____

_____

_____

_____

_____ / _____ / _____

"Lazy people do the minimum and expect great results. Great people do everything and still fear it isn't enough."

Anonymous

Priorities:

Spiritual Win	Mental Win	Physical Win

Today's Checklist:

☐ ☐ ☐

☐ ☐ ☐

I am grateful for...

1. _____

2. _____

Daily Reflection

_____

_____

_____

_____

_____

_____

_____

_____ / _____ / _____

"You have to believe in yourself when no one else does.
That's what makes you a winner."
Venus Williams

Priorities:

Spiritual Win	Mental Win	Physical Win

Today's Checklist:

☐   ☐   ☐

☐   ☐   ☐

I am grateful for...

1. _____
2. _____

Daily Reflection

_____
_____
_____
_____
_____
_____
_____
_____

_____ / _____ / _____

"If the ship doesn't come in, swim out to it."
Jonathan Winters

Priorities:

Spiritual Win	Mental Win	Physical Win

Today's Checklist:

☐   ☐   ☐

☐   ☐   ☐

I am grateful for...

1. _____

2. _____

Daily Reflection

_____

_____

_____

_____

_____

_____

_____

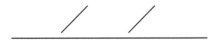

Today's Affirmation:
I release the need for validation from others and embrace my own self-worth.

Priorities:

Spiritual Win	Mental Win	Physical Win

Today's Checklist:

☐ ☐ ☐

☐ ☐ ☐

I am grateful for...

1. _____

2. _____

Daily Reflection

_____

_____

_____

_____

_____

_____

_____

_____

_____ / _____ / _____

Failure is not a sign of defeat, but a stepping stone
towards growth and success.

Priorities:

Spiritual Win	Mental Win	Physical Win

Today's Checklist:

☐ ☐ ☐

☐ ☐ ☐

I am grateful for...

1. _____

2. _____

Daily Reflection

_____

_____

_____

_____

_____

_____

_____

_____

Weekly Update

Goals for the Week:

☐ _____

☐ _____

☐ _____

What were your biggest accomplishments this week?

_____

_____

_____

_____

What areas could you have improved on this week?

_____

_____

_____

_____

_____ / _____ / _____

"I am the greatest. I said that even before I knew I was."
Muhammad Ali

Priorities:

Spiritual Win	Mental Win	Physical Win

Today's Checklist:

☐ ☐ ☐

☐ ☐ ☐

I am grateful for...

1. _____

2. _____

Daily Reflection

_____

_____

_____

_____

_____

_____

_____

_____ / _____ / _____

"The best revenge is massive success."
Frank Sinatra

Priorities:

Spiritual Win	Mental Win	Physical Win

Today's Checklist:

☐   ☐   ☐

☐   ☐   ☐

I am grateful for...

1. _____
2. _____

Daily Reflection

_____
_____
_____
_____
_____
_____
_____

_____ / _____ / _____

"The future belongs to those who believe in the beauty of their dreams."
Eleanor Roosevelt

Priorities:

Spiritual Win	Mental Win	Physical Win

Today's Checklist:

☐   ☐   ☐

☐   ☐   ☐

I am grateful for...

1. _____

2. _____

Daily Reflection

_____

_____

_____

_____

_____

_____

_____

_____ / _____ / _____

"Your time is limited, don't waste it living someone else's life."
Steve Jobs

Priorities:

Spiritual Win	Mental Win	Physical Win

Today's Checklist:

☐ ☐ ☐

☐ ☐ ☐

I am grateful for...

1. _____
2. _____

Daily Reflection

_____
_____
_____
_____
_____
_____
_____
_____

_____ / _____ / _____

"The expert in anything was once a beginner."
Helen Hayes

Priorities:

Spiritual Win	Mental Win	Physical Win

Today's Checklist:

☐ ☐ ☐

☐ ☐ ☐

I am grateful for...

1. _____

2. _____

Daily Reflection

_____

_____

_____

_____

_____

_____

_____

_____

_____ / _____ / _____

"Don't be afraid to give up the good to go for the great."
John D. Rockefeller

Priorities:

Spiritual Win	Mental Win	Physical Win

Today's Checklist:

☐   ☐   ☐

☐   ☐   ☐

I am grateful for...

1. _____

2. _____

Daily Reflection

_____

_____

_____

_____

_____

_____

_____

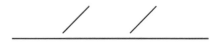

Today's Affirmation:
I am capable of overcoming any challenge that comes my way.

Priorities:

Spiritual Win	Mental Win	Physical Win

Today's Checklist:

☐   ☐   ☐

☐   ☐   ☐

I am grateful for...

1. _____
2. _____

Daily Reflection

_____

_____

_____

_____

_____

_____

_____

Weekly Update

Goals for the Week:

☐ _____

☐ _____

☐ _____

*What were your biggest
accomplishments this week?*

_____

_____

_____

_____

*What areas could you have
improved on this week?*

_____

_____

_____

_____

_____ / _____ / _____

"Success is not final, failure is not fatal: It is the courage to continue that counts."
Winston Churchill

Priorities:

Spiritual Win	Mental Win	Physical Win

Today's Checklist:

☐ ☐ ☐

☐ ☐ ☐

I am grateful for...

1. _____

2. _____

Daily Reflection

_____

_____

_____

_____

_____

_____

_____

_____

_____ / _____ / _____

"The greatest pleasure in life is doing what people say you cannot do."
Walter Bagehot

Priorities:

Spiritual Win	Mental Win	Physical Win

Today's Checklist:

☐ ☐ ☐

☐ ☐ ☐

I am grateful for...

1. _____

2. _____

Daily Reflection

_____

_____

_____

_____

_____

_____

_____

_____

_____ / _____ / _____

"Don't watch the clock; do what it does. Keep going."
Sam Levenson

Priorities:

Spiritual Win	Mental Win	Physical Win

Today's Checklist:

☐   ☐   ☐

☐   ☐   ☐

I am grateful for...

1. _____

2. _____

Daily Reflection

_____

_____

_____

_____

_____

_____

_____

_____ / _____ /

"If you want to go fast, go alone. If you want to go far, go together."
African Proverb

Priorities:

Spiritual Win	Mental Win	Physical Win

Today's Checklist:

☐ ☐ ☐

☐ ☐ ☐

I am grateful for...

1. _____

2. _____

Daily Reflection

_____

_____

_____

_____

_____

_____

_____

_____ / _____ / _____

"A comfort zone is a beautiful place, but nothing ever grows there."
Anonymous

Priorities:

Spiritual Win	Mental Win	Physical Win

Today's Checklist:

☐   ☐   ☐

☐   ☐   ☐

I am grateful for...

1. _____
2. _____

Daily Reflection

_____
_____
_____
_____
_____
_____
_____

_____ / _____ / _____

"You can't put a limit on anything.
The more you dream, the farther you get."
Michael Phelps

Priorities:

Spiritual Win	Mental Win	Physical Win

Today's Checklist:

☐ ☐ ☐

☐ ☐ ☐

I am grateful for...

1. _____
2. _____

Daily Reflection

_____
_____
_____
_____
_____
_____
_____

_____ / _____ / _____

Today's Affirmation:
I am resilient in the face of adversity and find strength in difficult times.

Priorities:

Spiritual Win	Mental Win	Physical Win

Today's Checklist:

☐   ☐   ☐

☐   ☐   ☐

I am grateful for...

1. _____

2. _____

Daily Reflection

_____

_____

_____

_____

_____

_____

_____

Weekly Update

Goals for the Week:

☐ _____

☐ _____

☐ _____

What were your biggest accomplishments this week?

_____

_____

_____

_____

What areas could you have improved on this week?

_____

_____

_____

_____

_____ / _____ / _____

"He who sweats more in training will bleed less in war."
Spartan Proverb

Priorities:

Spiritual Win	Mental Win	Physical Win

Today's Checklist:

☐   ☐   ☐

☐   ☐   ☐

I am grateful for...

1. _____

2. _____

Daily Reflection

_____

_____

_____

_____

_____

_____

_____

_____ / _____ / _____

"The only place where success comes before work is in the dictionary."
Vidal Sassoon

Priorities:

Spiritual Win	Mental Win	Physical Win

Today's Checklist:

☐　　　　☐　　　　☐

☐　　　　☐　　　　☐

I am grateful for...

1. _____
2. _____

Daily Reflection

_____
_____
_____
_____
_____
_____
_____
_____

_____ / _____ / _____

"You don't have to be great to start, but you have to start to be great."
Zig Ziglar

Priorities:

Spiritual Win	Mental Win	Physical Win

Today's Checklist:

☐ ☐ ☐

☐ ☐ ☐

I am grateful for...

1. _____
2. _____

Daily Reflection

_____

_____

_____

_____

_____

_____

_____

_____ / _____ / _____

"The only limits in life are the ones you make."
Anonymous

Priorities:

Spiritual Win	Mental Win	Physical Win

Today's Checklist:

☐ ☐ ☐

☐ ☐ ☐

I am grateful for...

1. _____
2. _____

Daily Reflection

_____
_____
_____
_____
_____
_____
_____

_____ / _____ / _____

"The harder you work, the luckier you get."
Gary Player

Priorities:

Spiritual Win	Mental Win	Physical Win

Today's Checklist:

☐   ☐   ☐

☐   ☐   ☐

I am grateful for...

1. _____

2. _____

Daily Reflection

_____

_____

_____

_____

_____

_____

_____

_____ / _____ / _____

"All hard work brings a profit, but mere talk leads only to poverty."
Proverbs 14:23

Priorities:

Spiritual Win	Mental Win	Physical Win

Today's Checklist:

☐   ☐   ☐

☐   ☐   ☐

I am grateful for...

1. _____

2. _____

Daily Reflection

_____

_____

_____

_____

_____

_____

_____

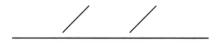

_____ / _____ / _____

Today's Affirmation:
I release fear and embrace uncertainty as a catalyst for personal growth.

Priorities:

Spiritual Win	Mental Win	Physical Win

Today's Checklist:

☐ ☐ ☐

☐ ☐ ☐

I am grateful for...

1. _____

2. _____

Daily Reflection

_____

_____

_____

_____

_____

_____

_____

Weekly Update

Goals for the Week:

☐ _____

☐ _____

☐ _____

What were your biggest accomplishments this week?

_____

_____

_____

_____

What areas could you have improved on this week?

_____

_____

_____

_____ / _____ / _____

"The only guarantee for failure is to stop trying."
John C. Maxwell

Priorities:

Spiritual Win	Mental Win	Physical Win

Today's Checklist:

☐   ☐   ☐

☐   ☐   ☐

I am grateful for...

1. _____
2. _____

Daily Reflection

_____
_____
_____
_____
_____
_____
_____
_____

_____/_____/_____

"If you want something you've never had, you must be
willing to do something you've never done."
Thomas Jefferson

Priorities:

Spiritual Win	Mental Win	Physical Win

Today's Checklist:

☐   ☐   ☐

☐   ☐   ☐

I am grateful for...

1. _____

2. _____

Daily Reflection

_____
_____
_____
_____
_____
_____

_____ / ___ / ___

"Opportunity dances with those already on the dance floor."
H. Jackson Brown Jr.

Priorities:

Spiritual Win	Mental Win	Physical Win

Today's Checklist:

☐   ☐   ☐

☐   ☐   ☐

I am grateful for...

1. _____

2. _____

Daily Reflection

_____

_____

_____

_____

_____

_____

_____

_____

_____ / _____ / _____

"Obstacles don't have to stop you. If you run into a wall, don't turn around and give up. Figure out how to climb it, go through it, or work around it."
Michael Jordan

Priorities:

Spiritual Win	Mental Win	Physical Win

Today's Checklist:

☐   ☐   ☐

☐   ☐   ☐

I am grateful for...

1. _____
2. _____

Daily Reflection

_____
_____
_____
_____
_____
_____
_____
_____

_____ / _____ / _____

"Conformity is the jailer of freedom and the enemy of growth."
John F. Kennedy

Priorities:

Spiritual Win	Mental Win	Physical Win

Today's Checklist:

☐ ☐ ☐

☐ ☐ ☐

I am grateful for...

1. _____

2. _____

Daily Reflection

_____

_____

_____

_____

_____

_____

_____

_____/_____/_____

"Hard work beats talent when talent doesn't work hard."
Tim Notke

Priorities:

Spiritual Win	Mental Win	Physical Win

Today's Checklist:

☐ ☐ ☐

☐ ☐ ☐

I am grateful for...

1. _____
2. _____

Daily Reflection

_____
_____
_____
_____
_____
_____
_____
_____

_____ / _____ / _____

Today's Affirmation:
I am grateful for all the lessons I have learned and the
experiences that have shaped me.

Priorities:

Spiritual Win	Mental Win	Physical Win

Today's Checklist:

☐ ☐ ☐

☐ ☐ ☐

I am grateful for...

1. _____

2. _____

Daily Reflection

_____

_____

_____

_____

_____

_____

_____

Weekly Update

Goals for the Week:

☐ _____

☐ _____

☐ _____

What were your biggest accomplishments this week?

_____

_____

_____

_____

What areas could you have improved on this week?

_____

_____

_____

_____

_____ / _____ / _____

"Opportunity does not knock, it presents itself
when you beat down the door."
Kyle Chandler

Priorities:

Spiritual Win	Mental Win	Physical Win

Today's Checklist:

☐   ☐   ☐

☐   ☐   ☐

I am grateful for...

1. _____

2. _____

Daily Reflection

_____

_____

_____

_____

_____

_____

_____

_____ / _____ / _____

"The best time to plant a tree was 20 years ago.
The second-best time is now."
Chinese Proverb

Priorities:

Spiritual Win	Mental Win	Physical Win

Today's Checklist:

☐   ☐   ☐

☐   ☐   ☐

I am grateful for...

1. _____

2. _____

Daily Reflection

_____

_____

_____

_____

_____

_____

_____

_____ / _____ / _____

"The secret of getting ahead is getting started."
Mark Twain

Priorities:

Spiritual Win	Mental Win	Physical Win

Today's Checklist:

☐   ☐   ☐

☐   ☐   ☐

I am grateful for...

1. _____

2. _____

Daily Reflection

_____

_____

_____

_____

_____

_____

_____

_____ / _____ / _____

"The difference between a stumbling block and a stepping stone is how high you raise your foot."
Benny Lewis

Priorities:

Spiritual Win	Mental Win	Physical Win

Today's Checklist:

☐   ☐   ☐

☐   ☐   ☐

I am grateful for...

1. _____
2. _____

Daily Reflection

_____
_____
_____
_____
_____
_____
_____

_____ / _____ / _____

"Failure is a detour, not a dead-end street."
Zig Ziglar

Priorities:

Spiritual Win	Mental Win	Physical Win

Today's Checklist:

☐   ☐   ☐

☐   ☐   ☐

I am grateful for...

1. _____

2. _____

Daily Reflection

_____

_____

_____

_____

_____

_____

_____

_____

_____ / _____ / _____

"The best way to predict the future is to create it."
Peter Drucker

Priorities:

Spiritual Win	Mental Win	Physical Win

Today's Checklist:

☐ ☐ ☐

☐ ☐ ☐

I am grateful for...

1. _____

2. _____

Daily Reflection

_____

_____

_____

_____

_____

_____

_____

_____ / _____ / _____

Today's Affirmation:
I am worthy of success and celebrate my achievements, no matter how small.

Priorities:

Spiritual Win	Mental Win	Physical Win

Today's Checklist:

☐   ☐   ☐

☐   ☐   ☐

I am grateful for...

1. _____

2. _____

Daily Reflection

_____

_____

_____

_____

_____

_____

_____

_____

Weekly Update

Goals for the Week:

☐ _____

☐ _____

☐ _____

What were your biggest
accomplishments this week?

_____

_____

_____

_____

What areas could you have
improved on this week?

_____

_____

_____

_____

_____ / ___ / _____

"Some people dream of success while others wake up and work hard at it."
Napoleon Hill

Priorities:

Spiritual Win	Mental Win	Physical Win

Today's Checklist:

☐ ☐ ☐

☐ ☐ ☐

I am grateful for...

1. _____

2. _____

Daily Reflection

_____

_____

_____

_____

_____

_____

_____

_____ / _____ / _____

"I've failed over and over and over again in my life.
And that is why I succeed."
Michael Jordan

Priorities:

Spiritual Win	Mental Win	Physical Win

Today's Checklist:

☐   ☐   ☐

☐   ☐   ☐

I am grateful for...

1. _____

2. _____

Daily Reflection

_____

_____

_____

_____

_____

_____

_____

_____ / _____ / _____

"Opportunities are like sunrises. If you wait too long, you miss them."
William Arthur Ward

Priorities:

Spiritual Win	Mental Win	Physical Win

Today's Checklist:

☐   ☐   ☐

☐   ☐   ☐

I am grateful for...

1. _____

2. _____

Daily Reflection

_____

_____

_____

_____

_____

_____

_____ / _____ / _____

Comparison steals joy, focus on your own journey
and celebrate your progress.

Priorities:

Spiritual Win	Mental Win	Physical Win

Today's Checklist:

☐   ☐   ☐

☐   ☐   ☐

I am grateful for...

1. _____

2. _____

Daily Reflection

_____

_____

_____

_____

_____

_____

_____

_____ / _____ / _____

"Perseverance is the hard work you do after you get tired
of the hard work you already did."
Newt Gingrich

Priorities:

Spiritual Win	Mental Win	Physical Win

Today's Checklist:

☐ ☐ ☐

☐ ☐ ☐

I am grateful for...

1. _____

2. _____

Daily Reflection

_____

_____

_____

_____

_____

_____

_____

_____ / _____ / _____

"The only limit to our realization of tomorrow will be our doubts of today."
Franklin D. Roosevelt

Priorities:

Spiritual Win	Mental Win	Physical Win

Today's Checklist:

☐ ☐ ☐

☐ ☐ ☐

I am grateful for...

1. _____
2. _____

Daily Reflection

_____
_____
_____
_____
_____
_____
_____

_____ / _____ / _____

Today's Affirmation:
I am constantly evolving and becoming the best version of myself.

Priorities:

Spiritual Win	Mental Win	Physical Win

Today's Checklist:

☐   ☐   ☐

☐   ☐   ☐

I am grateful for...

1. _____

2. _____

Daily Reflection

_____

_____

_____

_____

_____

_____

_____

Weekly Update

Goals for the Week:

☐ _____

☐ _____

☐ _____

What were your biggest accomplishments this week?

_____

_____

_____

_____

What areas could you have improved on this week?

_____

_____

_____

_____

_____ / _____ / _____

"Many of life's failures are people who did not realize how
close they were to success when they gave up."
Thomas Edison

Priorities:

Spiritual Win	Mental Win	Physical Win

Today's Checklist:

☐   ☐   ☐

☐   ☐   ☐

I am grateful for...

1. _____

2. _____

Daily Reflection

_____

_____

_____

_____

_____

_____

_____

_____

_____ / _____ / _____

"You are never too old to set another goal or to dream a new dream."
C.S. Lewis

Priorities:

Spiritual Win	Mental Win	Physical Win

Today's Checklist:

☐ ☐ ☐

☐ ☐ ☐

I am grateful for...

1. _____

2. _____

Daily Reflection

_____

_____

_____

_____

_____

_____

_____

_____ / _____ / _____

"I find that the harder I work, the more luck I seem to have."
Thomas Jefferson

Priorities:

Spiritual Win	Mental Win	Physical Win

Today's Checklist:

☐ ☐ ☐

☐ ☐ ☐

I am grateful for...

1. _____

2. _____

Daily Reflection

_____

_____

_____

_____

_____

_____

_____

_____ / _____ / _____

"Your life does not get better by chance, it gets better by change."
Jim Rohn

Priorities:

Spiritual Win	Mental Win	Physical Win

Today's Checklist:

☐   ☐   ☐

☐   ☐   ☐

I am grateful for...

1. _____
2. _____

Daily Reflection

_____
_____
_____
_____
_____
_____
_____

_____ / _____ / _____

"Small minds try to disparage your ambitions. but great minds will give you
a feeling that you can become great too."
Mark Twain

Priorities:

Spiritual Win	Mental Win	Physical Win

Today's Checklist:

☐   ☐   ☐

☐   ☐   ☐

I am grateful for...

1. _____

2. _____

Daily Reflection

_____

_____

_____

_____

_____

_____

_____

_____ / _____ / _____

"The difference between a successful person and others is not a lack of
strength, not a lack of knowledge, but rather a lack in will."
Vince Lombardi

Priorities:

Spiritual Win	Mental Win	Physical Win

Today's Checklist:

☐　　　☐　　　☐

☐　　　☐　　　☐

I am grateful for...

1. _____

2. _____

Daily Reflection

_____

_____

_____

_____

_____

_____

_____

_____

_____ / _____ / _____

Today's Affirmation:
I am open to new opportunities and seize them with
enthusiasm and courage.

Priorities:

Spiritual Win	Mental Win	Physical Win

Today's Checklist:

☐   ☐   ☐

☐   ☐   ☐

I am grateful for...

1. _____

2. _____

Daily Reflection

_____

_____

_____

_____

_____

_____

_____

Weekly Update

Goals for the Week:

☐ _____

☐ _____

☐ _____

What were your biggest accomplishments this week?

_____

_____

_____

_____

What areas could you have improved on this week?

_____

_____

_____

_____

_____ / _____ / _____

Embrace change and adaptability, for life is a constant
journey of growth and transformation.

Priorities:

Spiritual Win	Mental Win	Physical Win

Today's Checklist:

☐   ☐   ☐

☐   ☐   ☐

I am grateful for...

1. _____

2. _____

Daily Reflection

_____

_____

_____

_____

_____

_____

_____

_____

_____ / _____ / _____

"If you don't build your dream, someone else will
hire you to help them build theirs."
Dhirubhai Ambani

Priorities:

Spiritual Win	Mental Win	Physical Win

Today's Checklist:

☐   ☐   ☐

☐   ☐   ☐

I am grateful for...

1. _____

2. _____

Daily Reflection

_____

_____

_____

_____

_____

_____

_____

_____ / _____ / _____

"And the day came when the risk to remain tight in a bud was
more painful than the risk it took to blossom."
Anaïs Nin

Priorities:

Spiritual Win	Mental Win	Physical Win

Today's Checklist:

☐　　　　　☐　　　　　☐

☐　　　　　☐　　　　　☐

I am grateful for...

1. _____

2. _____

Daily Reflection

_____

_____

_____

_____

_____

_____

_____

_____ / _____ / _____

"Failure is only the opportunity to begin again, this time more intelligently."
Henry Ford

Priorities:

Spiritual Win	Mental Win	Physical Win

Today's Checklist:

☐　　　　　☐　　　　　☐

☐　　　　　☐　　　　　☐

I am grateful for...

1. _____

2. _____

Daily Reflection

_____

_____

_____

_____

_____

_____

_____

_____

_____ / _____ / _____

"The only way to discover the limits of the possible is to
go beyond them into the impossible."
Arthur C. Clarke

Priorities:

Spiritual Win	Mental Win	Physical Win

Today's Checklist:

☐ ☐ ☐

☐ ☐ ☐

I am grateful for...

1. _____

2. _____

Daily Reflection

_____

_____

_____

_____

_____

_____

_____

_____ / _____ / _____

"The only person you should try to be better than
is the person you were yesterday."
Matty Mullins

Priorities:

Spiritual Win	Mental Win	Physical Win

Today's Checklist:

☐   ☐   ☐

☐   ☐   ☐

I am grateful for...

1. _____
2. _____

Daily Reflection

_____
_____
_____
_____
_____
_____
_____
_____

_____ / _____ / _____

Today's Affirmation:
I am resilient and bounce back stronger from any setback or disappointment.

Priorities:

Spiritual Win	Mental Win	Physical Win

Today's Checklist:

☐   ☐   ☐

☐   ☐   ☐

I am grateful for...

1. _____

2. _____

Daily Reflection

_____

_____

_____

_____

_____

_____

_____

_____

Weekly Update

Goals for the Week:

☐ _____

☐ _____

☐ _____

What were your biggest accomplishments this week?

_____

_____

_____

_____

What areas could you have improved on this week?

_____

_____

_____

_____ / _____ / _____

"Only those who will risk going too far can possibly
find out how far one can go."
T.S. Eliot

Priorities:

Spiritual Win	Mental Win	Physical Win

Today's Checklist:

☐   ☐   ☐

☐   ☐   ☐

I am grateful for...

1. _____

2. _____

Daily Reflection

_____

_____

_____

_____

_____

_____

_____

_____ / _____ / _____

"The journey of a thousand miles begins with a single step."
Lao Tzu

Priorities:

Spiritual Win	Mental Win	Physical Win

Today's Checklist:

☐   ☐   ☐

☐   ☐   ☐

I am grateful for...

1. _____

2. _____

Daily Reflection

_____

_____

_____

_____

_____

_____

_____

_____

_____ / _____ / _____

"You gain strength, courage, and confidence by every experience in which you stop to look fear in the face."
Eleanor Roosevelt

Priorities:

Spiritual Win	Mental Win	Physical Win

Today's Checklist:

☐   ☐   ☐

☐   ☐   ☐

I am grateful for...

1. _____

2. _____

Daily Reflection

_____

_____

_____

_____

_____

_____

_____

_____

 _____ / _____ / _____

"Believe you can, and you're halfway there."
Theodore Roosevelt

Priorities:

Spiritual Win	Mental Win	Physical Win

Today's Checklist:

☐

☐

☐

☐

☐

☐

I am grateful for...

1. _____

2. _____

Daily Reflection

_____

_____

_____

_____

_____

_____

_____

_____

_____ / _____ / _____

"The only person you are destined to become
is the person you decide to be."
Ralph Waldo Emerson

Priorities:

Spiritual Win	Mental Win	Physical Win

Today's Checklist:

☐ ☐ ☐

☐ ☐ ☐

I am grateful for...

1. _____

2. _____

Daily Reflection

_____

_____

_____

_____

_____

_____

_____

_____

_____ / _____ / _____

"If you want to achieve greatness, stop asking for permission."
Anonymous

Priorities:

Spiritual Win	Mental Win	Physical Win

Today's Checklist:

☐   ☐   ☐

☐   ☐   ☐

I am grateful for...

1. _____
2. _____

Daily Reflection

_____
_____
_____
_____
_____
_____
_____

_____ / _____ / _____

Today's Affirmation:
I trust in my ability to make wise decisions
and take action towards my goals.

Priorities:

Spiritual Win	Mental Win	Physical Win

Today's Checklist:

☐   ☐   ☐

☐   ☐   ☐

I am grateful for...

1. _____

2. _____

Daily Reflection

_____

_____

_____

_____

_____

_____

_____

Weekly Update

Goals for the Week:

☐ _____

☐ _____

☐ _____

*What were your biggest
accomplishments this week?*

_____

_____

_____

_____

*What areas could you have
improved on this week?*

_____

_____

_____

_____

_____ / _____ / _____

"If you want to change your life, change your thoughts."
Anonymous

Priorities:

Spiritual Win	Mental Win	Physical Win

Today's Checklist:

☐ ☐ ☐

☐ ☐ ☐

I am grateful for...

1. _____

2. _____

Daily Reflection

_____

_____

_____

_____

_____

_____

_____

_____

_____ / _____ / _____

"A wise man learns from his mistakes, but a
wiser man learns from the mistakes of others."
Otto Von Bismarck

Priorities:

Spiritual Win	Mental Win	Physical Win

Today's Checklist:

☐ ☐ ☐

☐ ☐ ☐

I am grateful for...

1. _____

2. _____

Daily Reflection

_____

_____

_____

_____

_____

_____

_____

_____ / _____ / _____

Life is too short to hold onto grudges; choose
forgiveness and let go of bitterness.

Priorities:

Spiritual Win	Mental Win	Physical Win

Today's Checklist:

☐ ☐ ☐

☐ ☐ ☐

I am grateful for...

1. _____

2. _____

Daily Reflection

_____

_____

_____

_____

_____

_____

_____

_____ / _____ / _____

"It's never too late to be what you might have been."
George Eliot

Priorities:

Spiritual Win	Mental Win	Physical Win

Today's Checklist:

☐　☐　☐

☐　☐　☐

I am grateful for...

1. _____
2. _____

Daily Reflection

_____
_____
_____
_____
_____
_____
_____

_____ / _____ /

"The person who says it cannot be done should
not interrupt the person who is doing it."
Chinese Proverb

Priorities:

Spiritual Win	Mental Win	Physical Win

Today's Checklist:

☐   ☐   ☐

☐   ☐   ☐

I am grateful for...

1. _____

2. _____

Daily Reflection

_____

_____

_____

_____

_____

_____

_____

_____/_____/_____

"Don't be pushed around by the fears in your mind.
Be led by the dreams in your heart."
Roy T. Bennett

Priorities:

Spiritual Win	Mental Win	Physical Win

Today's Checklist:

☐　　　　☐　　　　☐

☐　　　　☐　　　　☐

I am grateful for...

1. _____

2. _____

Daily Reflection

_____

_____

_____

_____

_____

_____

_____

_____ / _____ / _____

Today's Affirmation:
I forgive myself for past mistakes and
embrace the lessons they have taught me.

Priorities:

Spiritual Win	Mental Win	Physical Win

Today's Checklist:

☐   ☐   ☐

☐   ☐   ☐

I am grateful for...

1. _____

2. _____

Daily Reflection

_____

_____

_____

_____

_____

_____

_____

Weekly Update

Goals for the Week:

☐ _____

☐ _____

☐ _____

What were your biggest accomplishments this week?

_____

_____

_____

_____

What areas could you have improved on this week?

_____

_____

_____

_____

_____ / _____ / _____

Time is precious; use it wisely and prioritize what truly matters to you.

Priorities:

Spiritual Win	Mental Win	Physical Win

Today's Checklist:

☐   ☐   ☐

☐   ☐   ☐

I am grateful for...

1. _____

2. _____

Daily Reflection

_____

_____

_____

_____

_____

_____

_____

_____/_____/_____

"The call to remain complacent will only grow louder until you silence it with a pattern of behaviors that leave no doubt about your mission."
David Goggins

Priorities:

Spiritual Win	Mental Win	Physical Win

Today's Checklist:

☐ ☐ ☐

☐ ☐ ☐

I am grateful for...

1. _____

2. _____

Daily Reflection

_____

_____

_____

_____

_____

_____

_____

_____

_____ / _____ / _____

"The only easy day was yesterday."
Navy SEALs

Priorities:

Spiritual Win	Mental Win	Physical Win

Today's Checklist:

☐ ☐ ☐

☐ ☐ ☐

I am grateful for...

1. _____

2. _____

Daily Reflection

_____

_____

_____

_____

_____

_____

_____

_____ / _____ / _____

"You have to expect things of yourself before you can do them."
Michael Jordan

Priorities:

Spiritual Win	Mental Win	Physical Win

Today's Checklist:

☐   ☐   ☐

☐   ☐   ☐

I am grateful for...

1. _____
2. _____

Daily Reflection

_____
_____
_____
_____
_____
_____
_____
_____

_____ / _____ / _____

"There is no elevator to success; you have to take the stairs."
Zig Ziglar

Priorities:

Spiritual Win	Mental Win	Physical Win

Today's Checklist:

☐ ☐ ☐

☐ ☐ ☐

I am grateful for...

1. _____
2. _____

Daily Reflection

_____
_____
_____
_____
_____
_____
_____

_____ / _____ / _____

"If you're not willing to learn, no one can help you. If you're determined to learn, no one can stop you."
Anonymous

Priorities:

Spiritual Win	Mental Win	Physical Win

Today's Checklist:

☐   ☐   ☐

☐   ☐   ☐

I am grateful for...

1. _____

2. _____

Daily Reflection

_____

_____

_____

_____

_____

_____

_____

_____

Today's Affirmation:
I embrace challenges as opportunities for growth and embrace the process.

Priorities:

Spiritual Win	Mental Win	Physical Win

Today's Checklist:

☐   ☐   ☐

☐   ☐   ☐

I am grateful for...

1. _____

2. _____

Daily Reflection

_____

_____

_____

_____

_____

_____

_____

Weekly Update

Goals for the Week:

☐ _____

☐ _____

☐ _____

What were your biggest accomplishments this week?

_____

_____

_____

_____

What areas could you have improved on this week?

_____

_____

_____

_____

_____ / _____ / _____

"The key to success is to start before you are ready."
Marie Forleo

Priorities:

Spiritual Win	Mental Win	Physical Win

Today's Checklist:

☐   ☐   ☐

☐   ☐   ☐

I am grateful for...

1. _____

2. _____

Daily Reflection

_____

_____

_____

_____

_____

_____

_____

_____ / _____ / _____

Surround yourself with positive influences
and people who lift you higher.

Priorities:

Spiritual Win	Mental Win	Physical Win

Today's Checklist:

☐ ☐ ☐

☐ ☐ ☐

I am grateful for...

1. _____

2. _____

Daily Reflection

_____

_____

_____

_____

_____

_____

_____

_____ / _____ / _____

"The pessimist sees difficulty in every opportunity. The optimist sees opportunity in every difficulty."
Winston Churchill

Priorities:

Spiritual Win	Mental Win	Physical Win

Today's Checklist:

☐ ☐ ☐

☐ ☐ ☐

I am grateful for...

1. _____

2. _____

Daily Reflection

_____

_____

_____

_____

_____

_____

_____

_____ / _____ / _____

"Be yourself, everyone else is taken."
Oscar Wilde

Priorities:

Spiritual Win	Mental Win	Physical Win

Today's Checklist:

☐   ☐   ☐

☐   ☐   ☐

I am grateful for...

1. _____
2. _____

Daily Reflection

_____
_____
_____
_____
_____
_____
_____
_____

_____ / _____ / _____

"Dream big and dare to fail."
Norman Vaughan

Priorities:

Spiritual Win	Mental Win	Physical Win

Today's Checklist:

☐ ☐ ☐

☐ ☐ ☐

I am grateful for...

1. _____

2. _____

Daily Reflection

_____

_____

_____

_____

_____

_____

_____

_____

_____ / _____ / _____

"You have to be willing to lose everything to gain anything."
Anonymous

Priorities:

Spiritual Win	Mental Win	Physical Win

Today's Checklist:

☐   ☐   ☐

☐   ☐   ☐

I am grateful for...

1. _____
2. _____

Daily Reflection

_____
_____
_____
_____
_____
_____
_____
_____

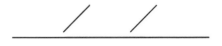

Today's Affirmation:
I am deserving of love, happiness, and success in all areas of my life.

Priorities:

Spiritual Win	Mental Win	Physical Win

Today's Checklist:

☐   ☐   ☐

☐   ☐   ☐

I am grateful for...

1. _____
2. _____

Daily Reflection

_____
_____
_____
_____
_____
_____
_____
_____

Weekly Update

Goals for the Week:

☐ _____

☐ _____

☐ _____

What were your biggest accomplishments this week?

_____

_____

_____

_____

What areas could you have improved on this week?

_____

_____

_____

_____

_____ / _____ / _____

Kindness costs nothing but has the power to change lives.

Priorities:

Spiritual Win	Mental Win	Physical Win

Today's Checklist:

☐　　　　☐　　　　☐

☐　　　　☐　　　　☐

I am grateful for...

1. _____

2. _____

Daily Reflection

_____

_____

_____

_____

_____

_____

_____

_____

_____ / _____ / _____

"Your work is going to fill a large part of your life, and the only way to be truly satisfied is to do what you believe is great work."
Steve Jobs

Priorities:

Spiritual Win	Mental Win	Physical Win

Today's Checklist:

☐   ☐   ☐

☐   ☐   ☐

I am grateful for...

1. _____
2. _____

Daily Reflection

_____
_____
_____
_____
_____
_____
_____

_____ / _____ / _____

"Learn as if you will live forever, live like you will die tomorrow."
Mahatma Gandhi

Priorities:

Spiritual Win	Mental Win	Physical Win

Today's Checklist:

☐   ☐   ☐

☐   ☐   ☐

I am grateful for...

1. _____

2. _____

Daily Reflection

_____

_____

_____

_____

_____

_____

_____

_____ / _____ / _____

"If you want to be great then you have to do what others won't."
Anonymous

Priorities:

Spiritual Win	Mental Win	Physical Win

Today's Checklist:

☐   ☐   ☐

☐   ☐   ☐

I am grateful for...

1. _____

2. _____

Daily Reflection

_____

_____

_____

_____

_____

_____

_____

_____ / _____ / _____

"To beat me, he's going to have to kill me. He's gonna have to have the heart to stand in front of me and to do that, he's got to be willing to die himself."

Rocky Balboa

Priorities:

Spiritual Win	Mental Win	Physical Win

Today's Checklist:

☐　　　　☐　　　　☐

☐　　　　☐　　　　☐

I am grateful for...

1. _____

2. _____

Daily Reflection

_____

_____

_____

_____

_____

_____

_____

_____ / _____ / _____

"The biggest adventure you can take is to live the life of your dreams."
Oprah Winfrey

Priorities:

Spiritual Win	Mental Win	Physical Win

Today's Checklist:

☐   ☐   ☐

☐   ☐   ☐

I am grateful for...

1. _____

2. _____

Daily Reflection

_____

_____

_____

_____

_____

_____

_____

_____

_____ / _____ / _____

Today's Affirmation:
I am worthy of self-care and prioritize
my physical, mental, and emotional well-being.

Priorities:

Spiritual Win	Mental Win	Physical Win

Today's Checklist:

☐ ☐ ☐

☐ ☐ ☐

I am grateful for...

1. _____

2. _____

Daily Reflection

_____

_____

_____

_____

_____

_____

_____

Weekly Update

Goals for the Week:

☐ _____

☐ _____

☐ _____

What were your biggest accomplishments this week?

_____

_____

_____

_____

What areas could you have improved on this week?

_____

_____

_____

_____

____ / ____ / ____

Be mindful of your words and actions, for they
have the power to shape your reality and impact others.

Priorities:

Spiritual Win	Mental Win	Physical Win

Today's Checklist:

☐ ☐ ☐

☐ ☐ ☐

I am grateful for...

1. _____

2. _____

Daily Reflection

_____

_____

_____

_____

_____

_____

_____

_____

_____ / _____ / _____

"Success is not the key to happiness. Happiness is the key to success. If you love what you are doing, you will be successful."
Albert Schweitzer

Priorities:

Spiritual Win	Mental Win	Physical Win

Today's Checklist:

☐   ☐   ☐

☐   ☐   ☐

I am grateful for...

1. _____

2. _____

Daily Reflection

_____

_____

_____

_____

_____

_____

_____

_____

_____ / _____ / _____

"The past cannot be changed. The future is yet in your power."
Anonymous

Priorities:

Spiritual Win	Mental Win	Physical Win

Today's Checklist:

☐   ☐   ☐

☐   ☐   ☐

I am grateful for...

1. _____

2. _____

Daily Reflection

_____

_____

_____

_____

_____

_____

_____

_____ / _____ / _____

"If you don't have confidence, you'll always find a way not to win."
Carl Lewis

Priorities:

Spiritual Win	Mental Win	Physical Win

Today's Checklist:

☐   ☐   ☐

☐   ☐   ☐

I am grateful for...

1. _____
2. _____

Daily Reflection

_____
_____
_____
_____
_____
_____
_____
_____

Practice empathy and seek to understand others before passing judgment.

Priorities:

Spiritual Win	Mental Win	Physical Win

Today's Checklist:

☐ ☐ ☐

☐ ☐ ☐

I am grateful for...

1. _____

2. _____

Daily Reflection

_____

_____

_____

_____

_____

_____

_____

_____ / _____ / _____

"Success is no accident. It is hard work, perseverance, learning, studying, sacrifice and most of all, love of what you are doing or learning to do."
Pele

Priorities:

Spiritual Win	Mental Win	Physical Win

Today's Checklist:

☐ ☐ ☐

☐ ☐ ☐

I am grateful for...

1. _____

2. _____

Daily Reflection

_____

_____

_____

_____

_____

_____

_____

Today's Affirmation:
I am enough just as I am, and I embrace my worthiness.

Priorities:

Spiritual Win	Mental Win	Physical Win

Today's Checklist:

☐　　　　☐　　　　☐

☐　　　　☐　　　　☐

I am grateful for...

1. _____
2. _____

Daily Reflection

_____
_____
_____
_____
_____
_____
_____
_____

Weekly Update

Goals for the Week:

☐ _____

☐ _____

☐ _____

What were your biggest accomplishments this week?

_____

_____

_____

_____

What areas could you have improved on this week?

_____

_____

_____

_____

_____ / _____ / _____

The greatest lessons often come from the hardest
experiences; embrace them and learn from them.

Priorities:

Spiritual Win	Mental Win	Physical Win

Today's Checklist:

☐ ☐ ☐

☐ ☐ ☐

I am grateful for...

1. _____

2. _____

Daily Reflection

_____

_____

_____

_____

_____

_____

_____

_____

_____ / _____ / _____

"The difference between ordinary and extraordinary is that little extra."
Jimmy Johnson

Priorities:

Spiritual Win	Mental Win	Physical Win

Today's Checklist:

☐ ☐ ☐

☐ ☐ ☐

I am grateful for...

1. _____

2. _____

Daily Reflection

_____
_____
_____
_____
_____
_____
_____
_____

_____ / _____ / _____

"Hard work without talent is a shame, but talent
without hard work is a tragedy."
Robert Hall

Priorities:

Spiritual Win	Mental Win	Physical Win

Today's Checklist:

☐ ☐ ☐

☐ ☐ ☐

I am grateful for...

1. _____

2. _____

Daily Reflection

_____

_____

_____

_____

_____

_____

_____

_____ / _____ / _____

"Rome wasn't built in a day, but they were laying bricks every hour"
John Heywood

Priorities:

Spiritual Win	Mental Win	Physical Win

Today's Checklist:

☐   ☐   ☐

☐   ☐   ☐

I am grateful for...

1. _____

2. _____

Daily Reflection

_____

_____

_____

_____

_____

_____

_____

_____

_____ / _____ / _____

Embrace authenticity and be true to yourself, for
that is where true happiness lies.

Priorities:

Spiritual Win	Mental Win	Physical Win

Today's Checklist:

☐   ☐   ☐

☐   ☐   ☐

I am grateful for...

1. _____

2. _____

Daily Reflection

_____

_____

_____

_____

_____

_____

_____

_____

_____/_____/_____

"Believe in yourself, take on your challenges, dig deep within yourself to conquer fears. Never let anyone bring you down."
Chantal Sutherland

Priorities:

Spiritual Win	Mental Win	Physical Win

Today's Checklist:

☐ ☐ ☐

☐ ☐ ☐

I am grateful for...

1. _____

2. _____

Daily Reflection

_____
_____
_____
_____
_____
_____
_____
_____

_____ / _____ / _____

Today's Affirmation:
I embrace change and see it as an opportunity
for growth and transformation.

Priorities:

Spiritual Win	Mental Win	Physical Win

Today's Checklist:

☐   ☐   ☐

☐   ☐   ☐

I am grateful for...

1. _____

2. _____

Daily Reflection

_____

_____

_____

_____

_____

_____

_____

Weekly Update

Goals for the Week:

☐ _____

☐ _____

☐ _____

What were your biggest accomplishments this week?

_____

_____

_____

_____

What areas could you have improved on this week?

_____

_____

_____

_____

_____ / _____ / _____

Cultivate resilience, for it will help you bounce back
from setbacks stronger and wiser.

Priorities:

Spiritual Win	Mental Win	Physical Win

Today's Checklist:

☐   ☐   ☐

☐   ☐   ☐

I am grateful for...

1. _____

2. _____

Daily Reflection

_____

_____

_____

_____

_____

_____

_____

_____ / _____ / _____

"In the middle of difficulty lies opportunity."
Albert Einstein

Priorities:

Spiritual Win	Mental Win	Physical Win

Today's Checklist:

☐   ☐   ☐

☐   ☐   ☐

I am grateful for...

1. _____

2. _____

Daily Reflection

_____

_____

_____

_____

_____

_____

_____

_____

_____ / _____ / _____

"Don't count the days, make the days count."
Muhammad Ali

Priorities:

Spiritual Win	Mental Win	Physical Win

Today's Checklist:

☐   ☐   ☐

☐   ☐   ☐

I am grateful for...

1. _____
2. _____

Daily Reflection

_____

_____

_____

_____

_____

_____

_____

_____ / ___ / _____

"The journey is worth it, even if the destination changes."
Paulo Coelho

Priorities:

Spiritual Win	Mental Win	Physical Win

Today's Checklist:

☐ ☐ ☐

☐ ☐ ☐

I am grateful for...

1. _____
2. _____

Daily Reflection

_____
_____
_____
_____
_____
_____
_____
_____

_____ / _____ / _____

"Happiness is not something ready-made. It comes from your own actions."
Dalai Lama

Priorities:

Spiritual Win	Mental Win	Physical Win

Today's Checklist:

☐   ☐   ☐

☐   ☐   ☐

I am grateful for...

1. _____

2. _____

Daily Reflection

_____

_____

_____

_____

_____

_____

_____

_____ / _____ / _____

"Sometimes it's the journey that teaches you a lot about your destination."
Drake

Priorities:

Spiritual Win	Mental Win	Physical Win

Today's Checklist:

☐   ☐   ☐

☐   ☐   ☐

I am grateful for...

1. _____

2. _____

Daily Reflection

_____

_____

_____

_____

_____

_____

_____

_____

_____ / _____ / _____

Today's Affirmation:
"I am confident, capable, and deserving of all the success
and happiness that comes my way."

Priorities:

Spiritual Win	Mental Win	Physical Win

Today's Checklist:

☐   ☐   ☐

☐   ☐   ☐

I am grateful for...

1. _____

2. _____

Daily Reflection

_____
_____
_____
_____
_____
_____
_____
_____

Weekly Update

Goals for the Week:

☐ _____

☐ _____

☐ _____

*What were your biggest
accomplishments this week?*

_____

_____

_____

_____

*What areas could you have
improved on this week?*

_____

_____

_____

_____

NOTES

NOTES

NOTES

NOTES